From Rags to Riches

A History of Girls' Clothing in America

• LESLIE SILLS •

For the
Billerica Public
Library—
Best wishes!
Leslie Sills

HOLIDAY HOUSE / NEW YORK

For Sylvia Sills, the proprietor, buyer, saleswoman, window dresser, and cashier of *The Pam Shop* in Manasquan, New Jersey (1953–1969); her sister, Ruth Stern, of *The Vogue Shop* in Asbury Park; and Ruth's sister-in-law, Renee Stern, of *Sterns* in Asbury Park—all of whom raced me around Seventh Avenue Midtown, New York City's Garment District, teaching me how to ask for what I want

—L. S.

Title page: Leslie Sills with her art students in Brookline, Massachusetts, photograph by Elsa Dorfman

Near right: Sylvia Sills (author's mother); Far upper right: Renee Stern (Ruth Stern's sister-in-law); Far lower right: Ruth Stern (Sylvia Sills's sister)

Acknowledgments

There are many people who helped create this book. Elizabeth Harding, my agent, thank you for believing in my vision. Mary Cash, my editor, your intelligent comments and ability to see the big picture was vital. All the people at Holiday House, I so appreciate your planning and checking. Ed Miller, you are a design genius. Sheryl Peters at Orchard House, Dr. Patricia Hills, Dr. Robert Oresick, and countless museum curators and librarians, particularly at the Boston and Brookline Public Libraries, were instrumental with research. I couldn't have written this book without consulting Joan Severa's scholarly book *Dressed for the Photographer.* I am grateful, too, to those who lent photographs: Goldie Doppelt, Pat Elliott, Susan Erony, Liz Geier, Dr. Salomon Grimberg, Milena Gostanian, Annie Kofke, Karen Moss, the McGloins, Larry Oresick, Gloria Pearson, the Stinys, Roger Schrantz, Emily Twadell, The Emma Willard School, and The Winsor School. Elsa Dorfman, thank you for your great generosity and spirit. Eric Oresick and Lourdes Santos, thank you for your support and love.

Library of Congress Cataloging-in-Publication Data
Sills, Leslie.
   From rags to riches: a history of girls' clothing in America / Leslie Sills. —1st ed.
      p. cm.
   Summary: Describes how clothing for girls in the United States has reflected society's changing views on children, from dressing girls as little adults in the seventeenth century to allowing girls to express themselves by choosing from a variety of styles in the twenty-first century.
   Includes bibliographical references and index.
   ISBN 0-8234-1708-5 (hardcover)
      1. Girls' clothing—History—Juvenile literature. 2. Girls' clothing—United States—History—Juvenile literature. [1. Girls' clothing. 2. Clothing and dress.] I. Title.

GT1730.S55 2004
391'.2—dc22   2003067600

ISBN-13: 978-0-8234-1708-7 (hardcover)
ISBN-10: 978-0-8234-2048-3 (paperback)

ISBN-13: 0-8234-1708-5 (hardcover)
ISBN-10: 0-8234-2048-5 (paperback)

Design by Edward Miller

Contents

Quilt from The Winsor School, Boston, Massachusetts, showing the history of girls' clothing there, from 1910 to the 1960s

Introduction

Clothes—we all need them to cover our bodies, keep us warm, and protect us from the weather. For some, clothes mean the latest fashions. Fashion magazines, newspaper advertisements, and television alert us to the "best dressed" and what they are wearing this season. Others don't care and buy only what's practical, a new pair of pants when old ones become too short or a new dress needed for a school event. Sometimes religion, politics, or cultural attitudes determine our clothing choices. An Indian girl may prefer a sari. An Amish girl will prefer "plain" clothing, as a Muslim girl may practice *hijab* and wear a head scarf. However little or much we think about our clothing, most of us want to wear what feels good—perhaps a certain soft fabric, a special color, or a design that allows us to move freely. Many of us want our clothing to reflect something about who we are. We buy T-shirts that advertise our favorite sport, celebrity, or personal philosophy. Back-to-school clothes may show we've changed or grown up. The perfect dress for that special occasion may say, "This is how I want you to see me."

Clothing *is* a form of communication. But until the 1960s, children's clothing mostly communicated their parents' position in society, as well as society's ideas about young people at that time. In 1860, a ten-year-old girl dressed in silk and velvet with ruffles and bows would most likely come from a wealthy family. Her mother would have selected the dress fabric, ornaments, and design, but her dressmaker would have done the sewing. Instead of comfortable undergarments, the girl would wear a tight-fitting *corset,* like a brace, to narrow her waist and keep her body straight. Looking "beautiful," she was also thought to be sweet, cheerful, courteous, kind, compliant, and never fussy or angry, especially in public. Dressing a daughter properly was a mother's job, which prepared her for marriage, becoming a mother, and running a household.

A well-to-do girl in 1860 may have been tutored or sent to a private school dressed in her everyday fine clothes. But a poor or orphaned girl, particularly from a city, might attend a charity school where she was required to wear a uniform. Parents and educators thought strict rules, physical punishment, and uniforms would give such a child the discipline and moral training she needed.

In New York City, children as young as three wore uniforms in infant schools, run by the Infant School Society.

Adults' attitudes toward *all* children influenced children's clothing, but when attitudes relaxed, boys benefited before girls did. Girls still had to dress like their mothers, in confining, sometimes even disfiguring clothes, long after boys were running about in comfortable outfits. Even in the twentieth century, when the first real play clothes were created for girls, the pressure to be pretty and clean was still enormous. In the twenty-first century, girls *seem* to have more choices. Yet with so many messages from the media and companies trying to create what will sell, selecting comfortable clothes that reflect oneself can be complex.

Swaddling and Stays

Confined Colonial Children

Childhood as we know it in the twenty-first century did not exist in Colonial America from 1600–1775. Adults did not think children were innocent, that they needed protection or even time to play. Instead, children were seen as little adults who were born sinful. Preachers advised parents to "break the will" of their offspring. Parents demanded obedience and commonly used whips and canes.

Because little was known at the time about health care, mothers often died in childbirth. Many babies died as well. And of those children who survived, more than half did not live past the age of five. With the average life span being only thirty years, children were rushed into adult life. Most began adult work between the ages of seven and nine. A poor child at age five might help support the family by working up to fourteen hours a day.

Colonial infants were swaddled, wrapped in layers and layers of cloth, usually *linen*. This made it hard for them to move. The tightly bound cloth held their bodies stiff. Doctors advised *swaddling* to prevent illness and keep limbs from bowing and bending into unnatural shapes. But parents thought swaddling was also a way to train their children to be good citizens. A straight body meant a high moral character.

In addition, swaddling slowed the heartbeat and made children sleepy, transforming crying babies into bundles that could be put out of the way, or even hung on wall hooks, so busy parents could work. It also kept parents from showing much physical affection to their children. Perhaps this protected parents from loving those who might not live long.

Toddlers, too, had to wear clothes that restrained them. Alice Mason, in the portrait bearing her name, stands tall and looks quite serious for a two-year-old girl. She wears a wealthy Colonial child's dress made of opulent fabric with ruffled cuffs and slashed sleeves.

Alice probably stands so straight because she has a built-in *stay* in her dress. Stays, used to support and shape a girl's torso, were stiffened with whalebone or strips of wood. Adults thought it feminine for girls to maintain an upright carriage with the help of stays. In diaries and letters of this period, girls talk about often having to sit erect for hours. Sometimes in school, teachers strapped girls to hard boards and put their feet in stocks to improve their posture.

> Jane Sharp, who wrote *The Midwives' Book* in 1671, stated, "Infants are tender twigs and as you use them, so will they grow straight or crooked." Sharp's warning became a popular saying, used well into the nineteenth century, that referred to children's moral development: As the twig is bent, so grows the tree.

In seventeenth-century Europe, clothing with slashes, such as Alice Mason wears in this portrait, was in style. The American Puritans, though, thought such clothing extravagant and enacted a law in Massachusetts allowing only one slash per sleeve.

Unfortunately, stays were unhealthy and sometimes even deadly. In 1665, two-year-old Elizabeth Evelyn suffocated when her stay broke two ribs, causing her undeveloped lungs to fail. Other girls died from stays as well.

Alice also wears a white *pinafore* over her dress, similar to the white aprons worn by Colonial women. Her loose-fitting, scarflike hood is an adult fashion too. Under her hood, she wears a cap, probably of linen, thought to protect young children from earaches. Children sometimes wore padded caps called *pudding caps,* as well, to prevent injury. Red ribbons tie Alice's sleeves. A strand of coral adorns her neck. Both the colors red and coral were thought to keep away evil spirits.

Sixty years later, in Schenectady, New York, a Dutch artist painted Susanna Truax. Similar to Alice Mason, Susanna is dressed like an adult although she is only four years old. She looks a bit less stern than Alice. Susanna wears a broadly striped dress with a wide skirt most likely made full with many starched *petticoats.* Since the bodice of her dress fits tightly and her waist is narrow, she is probably wearing a stay. Her loose-fitting sleeves with an extended drooping lace layer are a shortened version of *hanging sleeves.* Hanging sleeves were a style that evolved from the robes of sixteenth-century priests. In the seventeenth century, they were often used in children's clothing and reached the hem of a young child's dress. Like *leading strings,* cords or ribbons attached to the back shoulders of a toddler's outfit, they were held by an adult to help a young child move about without falling. Hanging sleeves and leading strings came to be associated, even in literature, with the idea of youth. Leading strings were sometimes sewn to an older girl's dress to show that she was still under her parents' guidance.

Susanna's shoes, with pointed toes and high heels, are a little like Dutch wooden shoes. Susanna holds a spoon with a piece of cake on it in her right hand and a flower in her left. Perhaps these images of sweetness and beauty indicate how attitudes toward children were starting to soften a bit.

Alice Shippen, a Colonial mother who sent her daughter, Nancy, to a finishing school, a place where she was to "finish" her life as a girl and get ready for womanhood, wrote to tell her, "Tell me how you improve in your work. Needlework is a most important branch of female education, and tell me how you improve in holding your head and shoulders, in making a curtsy, in going out or coming into a room, in giving and receiving, and holding your knife and fork, waking and setting. . . . These are absolutely necessary to make you shine."

Susanna Truax, 1730

Flowing Freedom

In the mid-seventeenth century, European and American religious leaders, philosophers, and educators began to question whether children were really born with a sinful nature. Some people believed that children were born pure, and they worried about the effects severe methods of discipline might have on them. An English philosopher, John Locke, wrote essays on this subject, which changed Americans' ideas. In his view, children should be held responsible for their actions only when they were old enough to understand them.

These new ideas did not change children's clothing, though, until the eighteenth century, when the French philosopher and author Jean-Jacques Rousseau began to write that children were divine creatures of nature. He thought they should be free to play, especially outdoors, and not go to school until they turned twelve.

Unfortunately, Rousseau did not think older girls were worthy of an academic education. Instead, he suggested dance, music, needlework, public speaking, and learning about plants and animals. Gardening and kite flying were his ideas of appropriate girls' sports.

Still, his writings led to a revolution in children's dress. Because he thought outdoor play so important, children's clothing was designed to be loose-fitting. Boys wore long pants. Girls wore free-flowing dresses, usually made of a lightweight fabric such as *muslin*, with a high waist, in what was called *Empire* style. When adults saw how comfortable these clothes

were, they copied them. It was one of the first instances in the history of clothing in which children's wear influenced adults'.

In *One Shoe Off*, a young girl wears a dress in the Empire style: with a low neckline, gathers at the chest, and a skirt that drops to a soft, natural shape. There are no stiff stays or starched underwear binding her waist or forcing her dress into a full shape. Under her dress, she is most likely wearing short, wide pants, perhaps made of *cambric*, a tightly woven cotton or linen fabric. Her short sleeves are tied up, making it easy for her to move and letting in some air.

Doctors, too, began to give new advice about clothing. Dr. Christian Augustus Struve, a German doctor and honorary member of the Royal Humane Society in London, thought confining children's clothes would cause a disease he called "ruptures." His opinions, as well as those of other eighteenth-century doctors, helped bring about more comfortable children's shoes. Children's buckled shoes gave way to soft pumps with laces.

> Dr. Struve exclaimed, "The dress of children should be different from that of adults. It is disgusting to behold a child disfigured by dress, so as to resemble a monkey rather than a human creature."

In *One Shoe Off*, the girl is allowed to relax and play, taking off one shoe.

Aprons and Calico

Gingham

In the early nineteenth century, 94 percent of Americans lived on farms. Farm girls wore simple clothes, dresses made of cotton, often printed in designs called *calico* or *gingham*. They wore aprons to protect their skirts as they helped their mothers preserve food and make candles, soap, shoes, and rugs. Bonnets with brims stiffened by starch, quilting, or cardboard inserts protected their faces and necks from the sun when they were working outside. These girls learned to spin and weave fabric to make clothes and bedding.

Farm girls and their mothers made cloth to sell as well. Businessmen would come to their homes to buy it and then resell it to country stores. Farm girls went to school only when they weren't needed to work on the farm.

Gradually, many women and their children worked together under one roof in a factory or *mill*. The first cotton-spinning mill made only thread. Samuel Slater, a mechanic from England, started it in 1793 in Pawtucket, Rhode Island. England controlled *textile* production at the time, but Slater memorized the plans for building his own spinning machinery and fled to America to find financial support. The first workers in his mill, called Slater Mill, were nine children, all under the age of twelve. By 1800, the mill employed one hundred children between the ages of four and ten.

In 1812, Frances Cabot Lodge Lowell designed a building in which cotton or flax could be made into cloth. There women and children worked *carding* the fibers with wire-toothed brushes to untangle them. Next came *spinning,* or twisting, the fibers into yarn. *Weaving* the yarn into cloth on

looms was the final step. The mill owners were particularly interested in employing girls, who, they reasoned, were not necessary on the farm. They thought girls' fingers were nimble. Plus, they did not have to pay them much. A poor or orphaned girl sometimes did not get paid at all. The mill owners were proud of themselves for keeping such girls' "idle hands" busy and out of trouble as they grew even richer.

With the invention of the cotton gin, a machine that removed the seeds and husks from cotton, in 1793 and the construction of the power loom in 1813, textile production moved from homes to mills throughout New England.

The below photograph, *Young Textile Workers,* shows

Aprons protect these young women's skirts, showing that they are working girls.

12

five mill girls from the Merrimack Manufacturing Company in Lowell, Massachusetts, one of America's first centers of textile manufacturing. The girls' clothing and postures say a lot about their lives. They look quite proper because they had to be. The girls lived in mill-owned boardinghouses run by mistresses, who enforced strict mealtimes, bedtimes, curfews, regular church attendance, and suitable clothing. Their dresses and aprons are plain, in solid colors, stripes, *plaid,* or calico. They sit or stand tall, with hands folded. Those sitting cross their legs. Their hair is pulled back so as not to get caught in the machines. Those whose feet we can see are wearing high laced leather boots. All wear collars. Some have pins. One wears a necklace.

Calico

Plaid

The Lowell mill girls took their jobs seriously. Their salaries, although not high, were good compared to those of other working women, 35 to 50 cents a day including room and board. But conditions were harsh. They endured seventy-three hours of work a week, in temperatures 95 to 105 degrees, with air heavily polluted by cotton fibers and deafening

noise in a room with 800 to 1,200 clanging machines. Still, in their spare moments, they started evening discussion groups; attended lectures, plays, and concerts; and even wrote their own magazine. Many saved their earnings and sent them home to help pay for mortgages and the education of their brothers. The Lowell mill girls, in fact, supported one quarter of Harvard University's all-male student population.

Agents of the mill would travel to the countryside to recruit girls. The girls would be picked up in stagecoaches, sometimes referred to as "slave wagons." In the South, where slavery *was* a part of life, the growing textile industry fueled the system. White landowners used their slaves to process cotton with the help of the new machinery. Slave women and girls worked long hours in plantation sewing rooms, spinning, weaving, sewing, and knitting. Yet slaves were usually allowed new clothes only twice a year.

Two women slaves, Judy Telfair Jackson, a cook for the Telfair family, and her granddaughter Lavinia. Both wear cotton dresses appropriate for their work. Lavinia's dress has irregular round shapes called spots.

One newspaper, the *Niles Register,* wrote that factory work was "better done by little girls from six to twelve years old."

Buckskins and Bishop Sleeves

All Sorts of Nineteenth-Century Girls

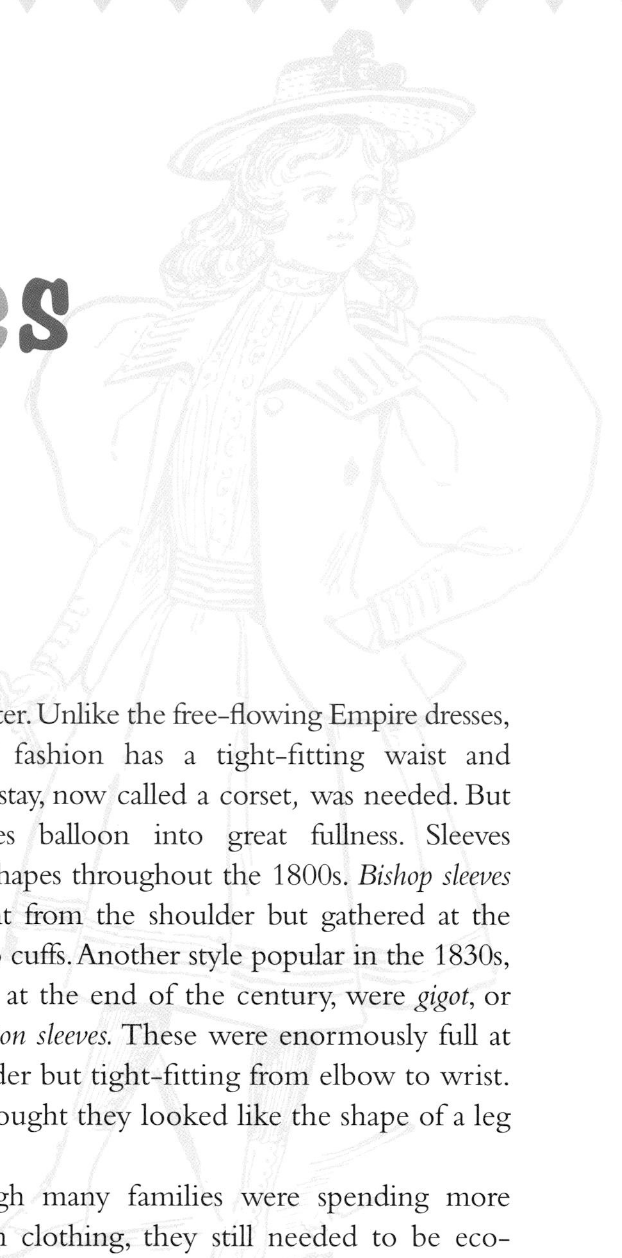

As the century progressed, the lives of middle-class American girls became more comfortable. By 1820, America's economy was rapidly growing. Many families moved into towns. Businesses were built, and the textile industry expanded. Middle-class women who once thought fancy clothes frivolous or even sinful now wanted them. Many ordered *fashion plates* from London and Paris and even sent to Europe for fabrics. Dressing daughters in expensive clothes became a way families could show off their success.

The green silk dress from England pictured here is one an American mother may have had copied for her daughter. Unlike the free-flowing Empire dresses, this girls' fashion has a tight-fitting waist and bodice. A stay, now called a *corset*, was needed. But the sleeves balloon into great fullness. Sleeves changed shapes throughout the 1800s. *Bishop sleeves* fell straight from the shoulder but gathered at the wrists into cuffs. Another style popular in the 1830s, and again at the end of the century, were *gigot*, or *leg-o'-mutton sleeves*. These were enormously full at the shoulder but tight-fitting from elbow to wrist. People thought they looked like the shape of a leg of lamb.

Although many families were spending more money on clothing, they still needed to be economical, especially if there were many children in the family. Dresses often had deep growth *tucks* that could be let out and wide hems that could be let down later. People wore clothes until the fabric was thin and then gave them to the poor—with all the trimmings, such as special buttons, lace, braids, and ribbons, removed. Less fortunate families sometimes took apart an adult dress, cut it down, and then sewed it to a child's size.

On the frontier, pioneer girls needed to be practical. They usually wore plain cotton dresses they

Above left: This skirt is made full with tucks. The low neckline matches earlier, more comfortable styles. Photograph © 2004 Museum of Fine Arts, Boston.

Above right: Leg-o'-mutton sleeves, 1895

could move freely in and wash easily. Sunbonnets and ankle-high leather boots protected them from harsh weather. Settlers often trapped animals to eat and, in cooler climates, used their fur for clothing. Pioneers also traded with Native Americans, and came to wear leather jackets, leggings, and moccasins made from *tanned* animal hides and sewn by Native American women. So many settlers wore fringed buckskin jackets that Native Americans

Above: Around this girl's shoulders is a blanket, most likely made of wool. Native Americans benefited from trading with the settlers and especially prized cloth and woolen blankets, having found that in wet weather, wool felt better next to the skin than leather.

called homesteaders "the fringed people." The fringes were thought to help rain drain off the garment.

Sweet Scented Grass, Twelve-Year-Old Daughter of Bloody Hand is a painting, shown above, of a girl from the Arikara tribe, also known as the Sahnish, who lived in the Missouri River Valley, in an area that is now part of the Dakotas. This girl wears a ceremonial beaded leather dress with fringe and beaded leggings. Her thick-soled moccasins are typical of the Indians from the Great Plains.

Left: A young woman identified only as Miss Barney, wearing leg-o'-mutton sleeves

Hoopskirts and Crinolines

Frilly Victorian Girls

As the country became more prosperous, people began to care more about their clothing and appearance. The invention of the sewing machine helped them look their best. Now factory clothing was made quickly and in great quantities. Families could make clothes easily at home, too, if they bought their own machines. Sometimes several families bought one machine and shared it.

Ladies magazines, such as *Godey's Lady's Book,* introduced in the late 1830s, promoted an interest in European fashions. Women all over the country and from every economic background read it. *Godey's* called the sewing machine the "queen of inventions." It published sewing patterns, as well as guides to cutting fabric, and even indicated the length of time it would take to machine-sew certain garments. Women who didn't sew or buy factory-made clothes hired a dressmaker or sent measurements with an order by mail to a city dressmaker.

Queen Victoria of England, crowned in 1837, greatly affected American styles as well. Although she was a monarch across the Atlantic Ocean, she had tremendous influence. American designers copied the queen's fancy, restricted clothing. Queen Victoria loved dresses with fitted *bodices* so tight that they required a corset. Her skirts were extremely wide, extended by underlying layers of *crinolines.* Crinolines, made from a layer of horsehair between two layers of cotton, were heavy and tiring to wear.

In 1866, *cage crinolines,* rows of flexible steel or bamboo hoops held together by cloth tape, replaced weightier versions. Cage crinolines were a relief, but still made it hard to move about. A girl wearing

Above top: In 1846, Elias Howe took out the first patent on a sewing machine. Six years later, Isaac Merrit Singer refined Howe's design by adding a foot pedal, and in 1889, his company added a motor.

Above bottom: Queen Victoria reigned over England for sixty-four years during a time when England was the most powerful country in the world. Courtesy George Eastman House.

hoops under her skirt might have trouble walking through a doorway, sitting down, or even using a bathroom. A strong wind could knock her over.

By 1850, girls were again dressed like their mothers, especially in public and for special occasions. The three girls in William Mathew Prior's painting shown below, *Three Sisters of the Copeland Family* (1854), are in typical dress-up outfits of the day. Necklines are off the shoulders. Waists are fitted and dropped a bit lower than one's natural waist, made possible by lightweight corsets. Skirts are wide and stand out with layers of starched petticoats or crinolines. The older girls wear narrow *pantalettes* that reach to the upper edges of their boots. The youngest sister wears striped stockings and *Mary Jane shoes,* also common for the times.

At mid-century, Americans could model their dress in photographic portraits. *Godey's* called the first photographs, known as *daguerreotypes,* "sun paintings." As photographic methods improved, many people were recorded in *tintypes* and *ambrotypes,* as was Mary Jane Field of Northampton, Massachusetts.

Crinolines could weigh fifteen pounds or more.

Above: Except for her ringlet hairstyle, Mary Jane Field, photographed in 1852, is dressed identically to the Copeland sisters.

Left: The father of these three well-dressed Bostonian girls was a successful black shop owner and a used clothing salesman, and their mother was a white Irish woman. When Prior, the artist and a supporter of abolitionists, painted the Copeland sisters, slavery had been abolished in New England but not yet in the South. Photograph © 2004 Museum of Fine Arts, Boston.

The lengths of girls' skirts once reflectd their ages. Skirt hems were always below the knee, but the older the girl, the longer the skirt.

Blooming in Bloomers

Liberated Girls of the Mid-Nineteenth Century

Covington, Texas, basketball team, 1920s

Some women despised dressing in fancy Victorian clothes. They didn't want to be stuck at home barely able to move. They wanted the same privileges as men, including comfortable apparel for themselves and their daughters. In 1849, Amelia Bloomer published a newspaper on women's rights called the *Lily*. Working with early feminists such as Elizabeth Cady Stanton and Susan B. Anthony, Bloomer spoke out against uncomfortable clothes that kept women from doing things men did. When Stanton's cousin Elizabeth Smith Miller came to visit in 1851, she wore a loose-fitting *tunic*-like top with soft, droopy, ankle-length pants, both of her own design. Stanton, who was pregnant at the time, adopted this comfortable outfit right away, calling it a "Turkish costume." Bloomer and other advocates of women's rights started wearing it too. In an 1852 issue of the *Lily,* Bloomer published a sketch and sewing pattern of the Turkish costume, the pants of which became known as *bloomers.*

Unfortunately, bloomers were thought by many (men in particular) to be unsightly and too radical. Newspaper journalists made fun of them. Women reformers reluctantly stopped wearing them after seven or eight years because they feared the fuss would distract from more pressing social issues, such as getting women the right to vote. However,

bloomers did catch on in the 1880s, when women became interested in exercise, skating, and bicycling. The Rational Dress Society, an organization formed in 1881, helped promote such clothing for active women and girls, calling it "healthier." Bloomers were worn well into the twentieth century in girls' gym classes.

New England high-school girls, 1897

Bustles and Ruffles

Stylish Girls of the Late Nineteenth Century

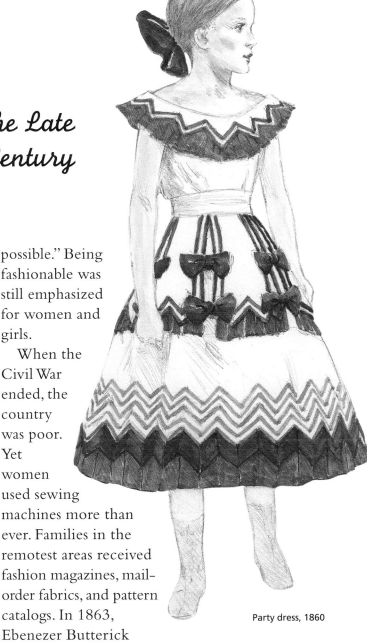

Party dress, 1860

In the 1860s, the Civil War forced families to make sacrifices. Cloth became scarce and clothes were expensive. In the South, cloth was recycled. Silk dresses became banners and flags. Women unraveled woolen blankets and knitted the yarn into mittens and socks. Petticoats were cut up for bandages.

In the North, women formed the Women's Patriotic Association for Diminishing the Use of Imported Luxuries. These women wanted everyone to refuse to wear fabrics from Europe, especially *velvets, silks,* lace, and fur. They considered anything extra, such as hair ornaments, artificial flowers, and feathers, extravagant and perhaps immoral. Hundreds of women, including the well-to-do, agreed and signed a pledge to boycott these luxuries.

American fashion magazines, however, seemed to ignore the war, with articles on and pictures of the latest styles. In the 1860s, children's fashions, such as this red-and-white silk dress with bows and ornamental rickrack, became regular features. *Godey's Lady's Book* printed paper dolls with ornate clothes, saying that these would help girls "to develop design, taste, and ability." Even in the West, where families made clothes from whatever was available, Jenny June, a writer for *The Prairie Farmer,* stated, "It's a woman's duty to be as attractive as possible." Being fashionable was still emphasized for women and girls.

When the Civil War ended, the country was poor. Yet women used sewing machines more than ever. Families in the remotest areas received fashion magazines, mail-order fabrics, and pattern catalogs. In 1863, Ebenezer Butterick started a highly successful pattern business that offered children's styles as well as adults'. For the first time, measurements were standardized, making it easier to sew clothes at home that fit. By 1871, the Butterick Company was producing 23,000 patterns a day and sold six million that year. Even Queen Victoria ordered them.

Pictured below, Josie and Lucey Schrantz, from Random Lake, Wisconsin, are dressed stylishly in "tunic dresses." A tunic is a long, one-piece outer bodice that fits over a second layer. Here the second layer is most likely a thin cotton under-bodice, similar to an undershirt, sewn to the skirt. Four layers of ruffles make the skirts full. Lace collars and cuffs and wide sashes add finishing touches.

The girls' curled hair lets us know this was a special occasion.

In 1861, Prince Albert, the beloved husband of Queen Victoria, died. For the rest of her life, the queen wore only mourning clothes, referred to as *mourning tweeds.* Dressed only in blacks, then grays, and eventually plums, the queen no longer influenced styles. Wide skirts narrowed. Instead, an innovation for thrusting out the back of the skirt (most likely thought to enhance the rear), called a *bustle,* became popular. A bustle was actually a cotton pad on a steel or cane frame. It was attached by hooks or laces to the waistband, under the skirt. While this new design was considered fashionable, the silhouette it produced distorted the female shape and looks comical to most people today.

In this tintype of three friends, two of the girls (on each end of the chain) wear coats with room for a bustle. The coats, probably made of wool, are long enough to cover the skirts' hems, indicating that the girls are approaching womanhood.

Dressed for the Party in a dress with a bustle, Chicago, 1874

Younger girls, from ages four to ten, generally wore more comfortable clothes. Their dresses became less full throughout the second half of the century. In the 1880s, waists dropped and a low sash was common, as in this printed pink-and-white silk party dress of 1883. Below, a Native American girl, from the Dakota tribes, wears a simple dress of a similar style. Made of cotton gingham, it has tucks in the front and a printed sash with a bow below the waist.

This dress is decorated with *pleats*, *rosettes*, and *smocking*, a popular technique in which fabric is gathered in a pattern with stitches. Photograph © 2004 Museum of Fine Arts, Boston.

A Dakota girl wearing European-American clothes, 1890.

Also at this time, people began to treat children more gently and with more care. Magazines now spoke of them as "lambs," "pups," "kittens," and "bunnies." Books were created just for children such as *Alice's Adventures in Wonderland,* written by Lewis Carroll in 1865, and *Little Women,* written by Louisa May Alcott in 1868. Two popular British children's book illustrators, Walter Crane and Kate Greenaway, drew characters in comfortable clothing that influenced styles. Greenaway's girls, in their high-waist dresses similar to the earlier Empire style, were featured in American fashion magazines.

A Kate Greenaway character

Many girls dreaded entering into a more adult life. Preadolescent Frances Elizabeth Willard, who went on to found the Woman's Christian Temperance Union, wrote in her diary of 1889, "This is my birthday and the date of my martyrdom. Mother insists that at last I must have my hair 'done up woman-fashion.' My 'back' hair is twisted up like a corkscrew; I carry eighteen hairpins; my head aches miserably; my feet are entangled in the skirt of my hateful new gown. I can never jump over a fence again, so long as I live."

Yoke Dresses

1900s

As the nineteenth century ended, rapid changes in America affected not only what people wore but also how they got their clothing. Department stores opened all over the country. For the first time, there were sections just for children's clothing. Mail-order shopping became popular, especially after the U.S. Post Office Department started its Rural Free Delivery system. There were catalogs and advertisements that featured only children's wear. All this made it possible for American girls around the country to wear the same styles. Many women continued to sew as well, ordering dresses as kits with linings, buttons, and trimmings. Even mothers who could afford to buy their daughters dresses sometimes preferred to sew them. Girls learned to sew their own dresses, too, in public school classes.

Dresses made by schoolgirls in Washington, D.C., 1899

Women began to be more independent. With inventions such as the telegraph and the typewriter, more women went to work outside their homes and wanted comfortable "work" dresses. More women played sports, too, some professionally, and needed "active" clothes. Such modern women wanted their daughters to have the same comfort and freedom. *Yoke dresses,* with fitted shoulders and gathers above

Girls learning to sew at school

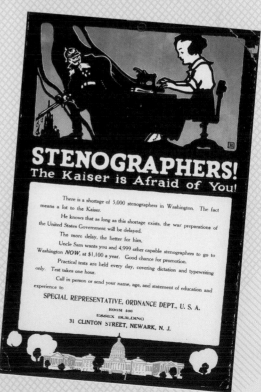

Above: High-school auto mechanics class, 1920s

Right: A poster recruiting women for government jobs

the chest, creating a free-flowing skirt without a waist, became popular for girls. Below, five-year-old Ethel Trottner wears a yoke dress with tiers of ruffles.

When there was a special occasion, though, girls and their mothers still dressed in confining "high-fashion"

Sisters Hannah Wilcox and Elizabeth Bancroft Smith in smocked yoke dresses, 1926

"The little woman of today is very sensibly dressed," stated *Ladies Home Journal* in August 1891. "Her hat shades her eyes, without being very weighty; her gown fits her prettily, and yet is not of a fabric so expensive that she cannot enjoy herself in it, and her coat is at once picturesque, and gives the needed amount of warmth."

Left: A loose bodice and skirt above the knee allowed Ethel to play freely.

Private-school girls in "high fashion"

clothes, such as those worn by these six girls from a private school. Although they certainly look spectacular in their generous bonnets, wide layered collared coats, fancy gloves, and lace-up boots, one wonders how pleased they are to be dressed in such cumbersome outfits. Magazines such as *Vogue* and *Ladies Home Journal* often dictated these styles for girls.

Near right: Mrs. Garland and her daughters, Constance and Isabel, a high-fashion family

Far right: Minnie Nosworthy, high-fashion girl, 1887

Shirtwaists

Immigrant Girls of the Late Nineteenth and Early Twentieth Centuries

In the late nineteenth and early twentieth centuries, millions of poor children were in desperate need of food and shelter as well as proper clothing. In cities such as New York, Philadelphia, and Chicago, immigrant families lived in dire poverty. The poor sometimes could not afford to care for their children. Babies were found abandoned on doorsteps, "dressed" only in newspapers. In the 1870s, there were more than ten thousand homeless children living on the streets of New York.

Poor children often had to become factory workers. By 1900, two million children were part of the workforce in the United States. Teenage girls in the clothing industry worked long hours, in miserable conditions, and for little money. Sometimes they had to pay to use the sewing machines as well as for electricity, needles, thread, and machine oil. Some had to buy their own machines and carry them to work strapped on their backs. Male bosses harassed the girls, locking them in rooms to work and allowing them to leave only for short bathroom breaks. If they were late or gone too long, they could be fined. Men worked in the garment industry, too, but as cloth cutters, managers, or factory owners.

The Triangle Shirtwaist Factory in New York City was one of the largest garment manufacturers. *Shirtwaists* were a popular style blouse in the early

Girls sewing in a factory

1900s. They were usually cotton, with full puffy sleeves, a high collar, cuffs, pleats down the front, and a fitted waist. The Triangle Shirtwaist Factory occupied the top three floors of a ten-story building. Like many other garment factories, it was badly maintained, with poor ventilation, broken windows, and many fire hazards. There, 240 girls sat in parallel rows sewing parts of each blouse. They sewed for more than ten hours a day. If they spoke to one another or sang, they were fined. The factory made fifty million dollars a year, but each girl earned only three to four hundred dollars a year.

Sweatshop worker

Wealthy matrons and college students, as well as working girls, including those in the factories, wore shirtwaists.

Clothing that was cut and assembled in a factory but still needed hand sewing was often sent to a *sweatshop*. Sweatshop workers were mostly teenage girls and unmarried women who had recently immigrated to America. Because a boss was paid for each article of clothing he returned to the manufacturer, he literally sweated out the work from his employees, demanding that they sew for twelve to fifteen hours a day. In New York City, there were six hundred sweatshops employing forty thousand workers.

Some of the girls and women of these factories and sweatshops were enraged by such abusive and unfair treatment. In 1909, with great courage, they organized other workers to strike for safer working conditions, fewer hours, and more money. They also wanted their union, the International Ladies' Garment Workers' Union, to be recognized.

The strike brought great hardships. Workers picketed for months without pay. Police arrested and fined striking women and girls and sent them to workhouses, prisons where they were forced to do hard labor. On some occasions the police or bullies hired by the companies beat them, sometimes breaking their ribs.

Surprisingly, not all New Yorkers knew about the strike. Because few workers spoke English, only

Yiddish and Italian newspapers covered the story. But one woman, Mary Dreier, changed everything. Dreier was the head of the Women's Trade Union League. This organization, formed in 1903, was made up of middle-class women who wanted to help create a better world. The very women who wore elaborate clothes with corsets and bustles and dressed their daughters similarly were willing to picket with the workers, set up soup kitchens, and offer funds.

On November 4, 1909, Mary Dreier was arrested while picketing the Triangle Shirtwaist Factory. At the courthouse, she had to give her address, which was in a fashionable part of Brooklyn. When the policeman realized she was a "lady," he was appalled at his "error." The *New York Times* heard about the case and put it on the front page. From that day on, strike reports were everyday news.

In December, the strike spread to Philadelphia, where more prominent women, such as Helen Taft, the daughter of the president of the United States, and Mrs. Gifford Pinchot, the wife of the future governor of Pennsylvania, joined the cause.

By February 15, 1910, some of the strikers' demands were met. Although not *all* companies recognized the union, the garment workers were granted a 52$\frac{1}{2}$-hour week. They also received a small pay increase and overtime wages, and no longer had to pay fines or rental fees. But even this success was short-lived.

On March 25, 1911, a fire broke out at the Triangle Shirtwaist Factory. The owners had never addressed the dangerous conditions in the building. There was no sprinkler system. The girls were trapped, as most of the doors were locked or opened inward. The fire escape quickly collapsed. Fire engines came, but could not help. Neither the ladders nor the hoses that the firemen brought could reach the upper floors. One hundred forty-six girls died.

This tragedy left a lasting impression on Americans. People were more painfully aware of the struggles of immigrants and, in particular, women and young working girls. Four years later, President Woodrow Wilson signed the first federal child labor laws, limiting the age and hours a young person could work. Through the next decades, more laws were passed to protect children's rights. School became compulsory. A juvenile court system was established to help abandoned, abused, and neglected children.

When women from wealthy families joined the garment workers' picket lines, people privately called them the Mink Brigade.

Flappers and Rompers

Modern Twentieth-Century Girls

1920s

In 1914, when American men went off to fight World War I, women replaced them in all kinds of jobs. The days of restrictive female clothing were over. By the war's end in 1918, women had shortened their hair and their hemlines. A style known as the *flapper dress* became popular for women and girls as young as seven. A long, straight bodice, either without a waist or with a dropped waist, and a hemline at the knee, made the "flapper look" free and easy. This loose-fitting style influenced girls' everyday and dress-up clothes throughout the country.

Girls in popular *middy blouses*, with wide collars and ties. All three have the new short hairstyle too, called *bobs*, 1930.

Above: High-school girls in flapper dresses

Far left: In 1924 in rural Pennsylvania, seven-year-old Mary Gernat wore a knee-length, flapper-influenced, white lace dress for her First Communion. Her veil reaches below the hemline, and her hair is short. White stockings and strapped shoes complete a modern-day version of a traditional costume.

Near left: Here Mary, without her veil, models with her younger sister, Olga. Olga wears a yoke-style dress, knee-high socks, and strapped shoes similar to her big sister.

Younger girls wore another innovation: the *romper,* or bloomer dress, also referred to as a sunsuit or playsuit. The romper was one piece, consisting of a sleeveless or short-sleeved top with short bloomer pants. The bloomer dress or romper let young girls move freely and get some sun. In 1927, scientists discovered that sunshine prevented rickets, a disease that hampers bone growth. Doctors encouraged mothers to put their children in the sun as much as possible.

Although wealthy girls still dressed in fancy silks, *taffeta,* and woolens, often imported from France, a more relaxed American style was becoming popular. Comfortable, simply designed, and inexpensive play clothes and dresses were now a part of the American way of life. When many Americans lost their jobs and savings in the Great Depression of 1929, sewing children's clothes became necessary. The Singer Sewing Machine Company began to

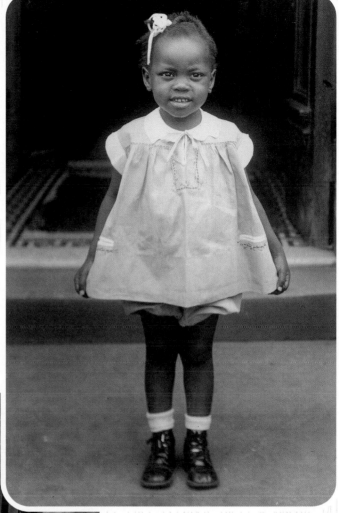

Above: Barbara Knight in a bloomer dress, 1928

Left: Playing in a middy blouse and bloomers, 1920s

sell machines on installment plans, allowing families with less money to pay a little bit each month over time. They also gave free advice on sewing techniques and dress standards. The United States Public Health Service sent sewing information to nurses, social workers, and public-school teachers.

Department stores hired nurses to teach shoppers about baby clothes. Educators told parents that all students must wear a new outfit for the first day of school. Simple styles in neutral colors were suggested. Girls were supposed to have six dresses with matching bloomers. Fussy shirtwaist blouses evolved into plain shirtwaist dresses worn by girls of many ages.

Psychologists encouraged parents to let children select their own clothes and dress themselves. They thought this would help develop self-reliance and

1920s

confidence. Designers created coats and jackets that children could take off easily by themselves. Recently invented zippers were sewn into everyday clothes, such as rubber rain boots, then called *galoshes.* Uniforms, now worn only in private schools, became unpopular because they didn't allow children to make their own choices. Girls dressed similarly only in gym class, where they wore *gymees,* bloomer-style gym suits with cushioned bottoms.

The shortage of cloth during World War I and the Depression led chemical companies to develop new types of cloth created with man-made fibers.

Rayon was invented as an alternative to cotton. It was soft and easier to produce. In 1939, *nylon* was considered a miracle. Durable and inexpensive, nylon replaced silk, particularly in stockings. The word "nylon" was a shortened form of "New York and London," two cities where its creators hoped it would sell well. Perhaps the idea to combine words came from a previous success, "Keds." Keds were the first *sneakers,* invented in 1917. The name was formed from the words "kids" and "*ped,*" the Latin root for "foot." Still selling today, Keds were sold by the millions, reaching a peak of six hundred million pairs every year in the 1960s.

Above right: Badminton team in gymees, 1934

Above: High-school girls in shirtwaist dresses

Right: Keds, the first sneakers

Shirley and Jane

Ideal Twentieth-Century Girls

Shirley Temple's innocent look, with dimpled cheeks, ringlet curls, and short dresses, created a standard for the perfect little girl.

Characters in children's books and movies also began to influence children's wear. Girls were dressed like Little Miss Muffet, Alice in Wonderland, and Minnie Mouse. The greatest influence, however, was child film star Shirley Temple. Born in 1928, Shirley was considered the "box office queen of the world." President Roosevelt said that Shirley Temple did more to brighten American spirits after the Depression than any other single person. In 1938, at age ten, her income was the seventh highest in the United States. Her signature dress had red and white polka dots with a curved, white collar known as a *Peter Pan collar*. It was mass-produced for girls of many ages in both expensive and more affordable versions.

America was a country of immigrants, and many wanted their children to be true Americans. Clothing that looked like what everyone else wore helped create an ideal. Well-dressed children were thought to be a sign of a mother's caretaking ability. Appearance began to be graded in schools. Teachers and administrators believed that children could learn more easily if they were wearing proper clothes. In the Dick and Jane reading books, used in grammar schools throughout the country from 1915 to 1965, Jane, like Shirley Temple, was a model of how an American girl should look. Always wearing a dress and seemingly immaculate, Jane helped popularize the idea that if a little girl is neatly dressed in a traditionally feminine way, she will also be well behaved, smart, alert, and hardworking.

Leigh and Annie Kofke, ideal twin girls in matching dresses with puffed sleeves and Peter Pan collars

Dancing girls, San Antonio, Texas, 1940

worn in previous years, she convinced her classmates every day at lunch, recess, and to and from school to sign a petition, which she then presented to their teacher. Her dream came true when she wore the pink, puff-sleeved *organdy* dress, with satin bow and lace trim, pictured here that she sewed herself.

When the United States entered World War II in 1941, Americans needed to be frugal once again. Knitting became common. Women made clothes from unusual sources, such as curtains. Some women used cotton sacks that had held flour, cornmeal, or animal feed. When manufacturers saw this, they began

After World War I, Americans saw children as the hope of the future and made it a priority to nourish them emotionally and intellectually. Dr. Benjamin Spock, the most influential baby doctor of the twentieth century, advised parents to listen carefully to their children because they had an inner wisdom. He said children naturally give cues about their needs, including what to wear. Girls were still expected to be neat, clean, and traditionally feminine, but they were given more choices.

In 1941, an eighth grader named Rita Rappoport from Public School 95 in the Bronx organized her class to ask for the right to wear fancy graduation dresses. Tired of the plain dresses

Dorothy Overall's prize-winning flour-sack dress

A fancy graduation dress worn at P.S. 95, 1941

Girls making clothes from sugar bags

to print sacks in appealing colors and designs. There was even a National Cotton Bag Sewing Contest, which Dorothy Overall, a Kansas wheat farmer, won in 1959 for her flour-sack dress.

Blue jeans became fashionable. The word "jeans" comes from work clothes made of heavy cotton twill clothing that was milled in Genoa, Italy. French weavers called the clothes "*Gênes,*" referring

A family in blue jeans in a painting by Susan Erony titled *1953*

to Genoa. But blue jeans came to the United States through Levi Strauss. Strauss was an immigrant shopkeeper who peddled his dry goods from the East Coast to San Francisco during the Gold Rush in the 1850s. He sold canvas to miners for tents, but when he saw how quickly miners' pants wore out, he started manufacturing pants in the heavy-duty canvas. A short while later, realizing that these pants would feel better in a softer material, he found a supple, durable cloth that was originally manufactured in Nîmes, France, known in Europe as "*serge de Nîmes.*" The cloth "*de Nîmes,*" then dyed blue to hide stains, became *denim*. In 1935, blue jeans were first shown in *Vogue* magazine as "western chic."

Following World War II, between 1940 and 1965, the number of children in America age five through fourteen doubled. People called it a baby boom. Americans were now wealthier than they had ever been. This financial security provided more leisure time. Families wore lots of play clothes.

Skiing in the West, 1950s

Girls, such as those in this eighth-grade gym class from Alamosa, Colorado, wore *Bermuda shorts,* 1941.

Many families moved outside cities to new suburban communities. A close-knit family where a father went to work and a mother stayed home with the children was considered ideal. Daughters were supposed to act and dress in a "ladylike" manner. Popular television shows supported this view, as did the Barbie doll, created in 1959. Barbie, with an unrealistic body, pointed feet that fit only into high-heeled shoes, and a wardrobe of fancy dresses,

served as a model of womanhood. Girls were not allowed to wear pants to school. Instead they wore dresses with pinafores and strapped sandals with ankle socks called *anklets*. The sisters pictured here, Barbara and Michele, wore *tartan plaid* skirts with matching sweaters, anklets, and *T-strap shoes* for a special occasion. Fancy decorations such as bows,

Whip up a seam in a wink!
Whiz through dolly's darning!
Even mend and sew your own
clothes with this lively machine
that makes sewing really fun

The Sister Electric Portable

SOLD ONLY AT SEARS $19⁷⁷

- Foot pedal and hand-operated control
- Portable machine weighs just 7½ lbs
- Sturdy plastic case . . snap-on cover
- Aluminum head, heavy-duty motor

The little seamstress will whip up the late fashions on this chain-stitching portable. It's an easy-to-handle 11x9 in. high a has a built-in light, knob-adjusted thre tension, storage drawer and cover with ha dle for toting or storing.
The Sister has a seam guide for straig sewing, pincushion, extra needles, threa and instructions. Long, 6-foot cord. U listed for 110-120-v., 60-c. AC. From Japa Buy it the easy way—order by phone.
49 N 1201—Shpg. wt. 7 lbs. 8 oz . . . $19.

Five Extra Needles. Sister portable on
49 N 1225—Shpg. wt. 2 oz. . . . . . Pkg. 3

SAVE THIS CATALOG
You can order toys on
pages 433 to 609
until August 1, 1968

Bobbin-type Sewing Machine

Sews lock-stitch that won't ravel $15⁹⁹ without batteries

Sturdy die-cast aluminum head . . sews with steady battery power. And the stitches you make won't pull out easily. Features an adjustable stitch regulator and bobbin winder. Plastic storage case, metal base. 9½x8 in. high. With extra needles. From Japan. Uses 3 "D" batteries; order 2 pkgs. below.
49 N 1261—Shpg. wt. 5 lbs. 8 oz. $15.99
Alkaline "D" Batteries. Package of 2.
49N4653—Shpg. wt. 10 oz. Pkg. $1.39

570 Sears BKMG

"Sew-Big" Outfit

Seat is storage hassock. $9⁹⁹ sew-table converts to desk

Everything your child will need for junior sewing projects . . patterns, appliques, thread, needles, thimbles, buttons, sew guide, ruler, tape measure, scissors and instruction book.
Hand-operated chain-stitch machine is die-cast metal, 7 in. long. Plastic sew-table . . platform folds under to form desk. Hassock 13 in. high . . . sturdy plastic with removable seat top.
79 N 1395C—Wt. 12 lbs. . . . $9.99

Hand-operated Sewing Machine

Beginner's Chain-stitch Machine $4⁴⁹

1 Features finger-guarding presser foot, adjustable thread tension. Die-cast steel head, 8xf in. high . . clamps to any table top. Uses standa rotary needles No. 24x1. Needles, thread, instructio
49 N 1250—Shipping weight 1 lb. 8 oz. . . . $4.

Advanced Chain-stitch Machine $6⁹⁷

2 Extension table holds fabric. Hardwood ba has storage drawer. Die-cast steel head and f ger-guarding presser foot. 12x5x7 in. high . . clam to any table top. Needles, thread and instructio included. Uses standard rotary needles No. 24:
49 N 1221—Shipping wt. 2 lbs. 8 oz. . . . . . $6.

NOTE: Machines (1) and (2) are from West Germa

Above left: Girls could also order toy sewing machines so they could sew just like their mothers.

Above right: Barbara and Michele Wallace modeling for a special event, 1962

embroidery, sequins, and appliqués were commonly added to girls' clothing. Poodle dog appliqués were in such demand that poodle skirts became a fashion category.

Teenage girls wore close-fitting sweaters with full or pleated plaid or *tweed* woolen skirts. *Saddle shoes,* laced shoes in two colors, usually brown and white, completed the outfit with cuffed socks called *bobby socks.* This look was so popular that teenagers came to be called bobby-soxers.

A poodle skirt, 1950s and 1960s

Girls properly dressed for play. Karen Moss, on the right, wears a pinafore dress.

A bobby-soxer, 1950s

Anything Goes

In the 1960s, teenagers and young adults rebelled. They questioned the values of the earlier generation. Girls were no longer willing to dress as adults thought they should. They had their own ideas about clothes, and the garment industry supported them. The youth market became big business. Clothing, especially for girls and teens, was mass-produced as it had never been before.

New fabrics were invented, such as *Lycra* and *Orlon,* that stretched and allowed for greater movement. Girls could run and jump however they liked in stretch tights and soft *corduroy.* This new physical freedom reflected a freer attitude about girls' behavior. They no longer had to be "proper." By the late 1960s, girls could wear pants every day.

Above: Milena Gostanian in a minidress, 1969

Right: Playing in newly created stretch fabrics, 1966–1967

Many other barriers were broken. Rules of modesty changed. Girls began to wear two-piece bathing suits, such as *bikinis*. Clothing of many nations influenced textiles. Printed fabrics from Africa and India were used for skirts, blouses, shorts, and dresses. Sports and leisure clothes became unisex, or appropriate for girls *and* boys. Styles were manufactured in many fabrics and price ranges, letting girls from all economic backgrounds look fashionable.

More and more parents allowed their daughters to make their own decisions, including their own fashion choices. Throughout the next decades, whatever new style manufacturers presented—*bell-bottom* jeans; long, flowered *flannel* "granny dresses"; miniskirts; preppy styles; layered looks; athletic wear—girls could pick and choose how they wanted to look. There was no longer one way to be.

Above: Teens Veronica Santo, Mary Adams, and Milena Gostanian in bell-bottom jeans and *midriff tops*, 1960s

Right: High-school girls modeling for a benefit called Teenage Consumer a Go-Go, 1967

At the end of the twentieth century, television, magazines, and newspapers began to avidly follow the dress of celebrities, showing images of models, actresses, and musicians often "barely" dressed. Teenagers and girls wanted to look "glamorous" like those women. A provocative clothing style, perhaps started by the Barbie doll, became a regular part of girls' lives. Whereas in previous decades, dressing girlish meant wearing youthful and innocent styles, girls now were given a different message about what was feminine. Although girls of earlier centuries were *forced* to dress like women, girls began to dress like adults on their own.

Garment manufacturers fed this trend. Large clothing companies didn't always worry about what would be healthy or comfortable for girls. Sometimes they didn't worry about the conditions of their workers either. Some American companies moved businesses to poor countries, where they could pay workers low wages. Often they used local factories, where it was difficult to monitor working conditions. Conditions could be similar to those faced by the immigrants at the turn of the twentieth century in America.

Today, many of these conditions still exist. But girls don't have to bother with fashions they think look silly or are uncomfortable. Nor do they have to support companies who hire children or take advantage of their workers.

Pictured here, Lally and Mardet wear outfits that reflect the tastes and needs of savvy girls. Both wear loose-fitting pants that allow them to move freely but still look stylish. Their T-shirts, made of soft cotton, have flower appliqués that show their femininity. Mardet's pants have a matching flower appliqué. Her shirtsleeves repeat the flower pattern. Lally wears a jacket made of sweatshirt material with snaps for easy opening and closing. Both girls wear shoes with laces in which they can run, jump, or just walk.

Also pictured here, Catherine wears an outfit that would make Tinkerbell jealous. Made by her grandmother, this dress is part fairy costume, part bumblebee, and part budding flower. Metallic blue-

Lally and Mardet wear comfortable play clothes.

Catherine in a fantasy delight

Above left: Lucia's design drawing that became a dress for both her and her mom

Above center: Lucia's drawing of her creation, the yin-yang dress

Above right: Lucia modeling her yin-yang dress

and-silver shoes with clear tops let her toes peek through. A grand pink satin hat trimmed with white feathers and lace frames her face and adds a finishing special touch. It is a play outfit that shows the delight a young girl can have when what she is wearing matches her imagination.

At age six, a Californian girl named Lucia was so determined to have her clothes match her imagination that she began *drawing* what she wanted to wear. After Lucia had designed clothes for various seasons, impressing all those who saw them, her mother hired a dressmaker, Liz Geier, to sew her daughter's fantasies. Lucia calls this black-and-white style her yin-yang dress. Her green-and-blue

striped design became a dress not only for her but for her mother as well. Lucia's friends then wanted to design their own clothes and began drawing too. Taken with the originality of the girls' designs, Liz Geier started a clothing company called Imagine This . . . , producing each girl's design. Now girls can have their fashion fantasies become a reality. Imagine This . . . shows what can happen when girls are given support for their creative efforts.

While clothing may still reflect many aspects of society—social attitudes, war or peacetime conditions, the economy, and new technologies—girls can choose clothes that celebrate themselves. They can be their own designers, creating *their* styles—and lives.

To the Readers

Fashion statements are as varied as people. Flowing dresses, ethnic costumes, and designer jeans may be dress-up or school clothes depending on who is doing the choosing. While our clothing is not the ultimate reflection of who we are, we can choose different styles for our moods, occasions, and ages.

We can also be particular as consumers and support only companies that maintain fair labor practices. Several organizations monitor the garment industry and can tell you which companies are best taking care of their employees. Large corporations often hire small factories in foreign countries to sew their clothing. Sometimes it is difficult to check on them, but not impossible.

An organization called UNITE has a website (www.UNITEunion.org) devoted to young people. There you can send a letter to the director of the International Labor Organization to voice your concerns. You can even send poetry and artwork and read and see that of other young people. UNITE's website will also lead you to sites for the National Labor Committee, the Campaign for Labor Rights, and Co-op America, organizations that make suggestions and give reports on the garment industry to help you make wise choices.

Fashion can be fun. And the history of girls' clothing tells a lot about who we are and from where we have come. What girls decide to wear, buy, design, advertise, or ignore will determine the fashions of the future.

Glossary

ambrotypes: Early types of photographs that captured likenesses on a glass negative backed by a dark surface.

anklets: Socks that end at the ankle.

bell-bottoms: Pants, often made of denim, that are narrow at the knee but fan out to form a bell shape at the lower leg; popular in the 1970s.

Bermuda shorts: Short pants for leisure wear that end above the knee; introduced in the 1950s.

bikinis: Two-piece bathing suits for girls and women, often cut briefly at the breasts and low at the hips; introduced in the 1960s.

bishop sleeves: A sleeve style in which a long sleeve falls straight from the shoulder but gathers into a cuff at the wrist; popular in the 1800s.

bloomers: Wide, loose pants that originally gathered at the ankle and were worn under skirts. Later referred to full, billowy pants gathered at any length. Named after suffragette Amelia Bloomer but designed by Elizabeth Smith Miller, cousin of Elizabeth Cady Stanton, in 1851.

blue jeans: Named from work clothes crafted from a heavy cotton milled in Genoa, Italy, and called *Gênes* by French weavers. Came to America in the 1850s through Levi Strauss, who created similar heavy-duty pants for miners during the Gold Rush.

bobby socks: Thick, cuffed socks often worn in the 1950s by teenagers, who were then sometimes referred to as bobby-soxers.

bobs: Short hairstyles with hair one length and curls curved over the ears toward the cheeks. Worn by flappers; popular in the 1920s.

bodices: The part of dresses that extends from the shoulders to the waist.

bustle: A cotton pad mounted on a steel or cane frame, then attached by hooks or laces to a waistband under a skirt. Popular in the late nineteenth century, the bustle thrust out the back of a dress, creating a bulge considered attractive.

cage crinolines: Series of steel or bamboo hoops held together by cloth tape and worn under skirts in the mid-nineteenth century to create fullness.

calico: Printed cotton cloth, usually in a design of small flowers.

cambric: Tightly woven lightweight cotton or linen fabric.

carding: The disentangling of fibers with a wire toothed brush or a machine with rows of wire teeth.

corduroy: A durable cotton material with vertical raised lines of fabric.

corset: A nineteenth-century, close-fitting female undergarment, often made stiff with whalebone or strips of wood. Used since medieval times, when it was called a stay, to narrow the waist, accentuate the breasts and hips, and hold the body stiff.

crinolines: Slips worn under skirts to widen them. In the nineteenth century, crinolines were made of a layer of stiff horsehair between two layers of cotton.

daguerreotypes: Early types of photographs in which images were created on a light-sensitive, silver-coated metallic plate.

denim: A tough, cotton cloth dyed blue and often used for jeans and work clothes. The name evolved from the phrase *de Nîmes* (of Nîmes), since a similar cloth originally came from Nîmes, France.

Empire dress: A style popular in the early nineteenth century featuring a low neckline, short sleeves, gathers under the breasts, and a free-flowing skirt.

fashion plates: Magazine illustrations showing the latest styles.

flannel: A soft, brushed fabric made of cotton, wool, synthetic (man-made) fibers, or a combination of these. Often used today for sleepwear.

flapper dress: A style of dress started in the 1920s, consisting of a loose-fitting bodice with a dropped waist or no waist and a skirt ending at the knee. Women who wore this style were called flappers.

galoshes: Waterproof overshoes or rubber boots.

gigot: A leg-o'-mutton sleeve (*see* below).

gingham: A cotton fabric woven in solid colors, checks, stripes, or plaid, although known mostly in checks.

gymees: Girls' gym suits worn in the 1920s and 1930s, with bloomer pants and cushioned bottoms for protection against falls.

hanging sleeves: A sleeve style originating from the robes of sixteenth-century priests. In the seventeenth century and later, hanging sleeves reached as long as the hem of a young child's dress and were used to guide a child's movement. They became a symbol referring to youth.

hijab: A way of dressing practiced by Muslim women in which they cover their heads and bodies with cloth, exposing only their eyes.

Keds: The first rubber-soled canvas shoes, or sneakers, invented in 1917. The name combines the words "kids" and "*ped*," the Latin root for "foot."

leading strings: Strings or cords sewn to the shoulders of a toddler's clothing for an adult to hold and guide the child's movement. Used since medieval times, but seen into the nineteenth century on young girls' dresses to indicate that they were still under their parents' guidance.

leg-o'-mutton sleeves: First seen in 1830, a sleeve shape that is full and puffy at the shoulder and narrow and tight from the elbow to the wrist, thought to resemble the shape of a leg of lamb.

linen: A fabric made from the fibers of the flax plant.

Lycra: A stretchy, synthetic (man-made) fabric invented in 1958.

Mary Janes: A female shoe style consisting of a round toe and a strap that buckles across the top part of the foot, most often in black, especially shiny black patent leather.

middy blouses: Popular blouses in the early twentieth century that were loose fitting with a sailor collar and tie, commonly in white with a navy blue tie.

midriff tops: Tops worn by girls and women in which the area below the breasts and above the waist is exposed.

mill: A building with machinery for manufacturing; a factory.

mourning tweeds: The dark clothing of Queen Victoria worn after the death of her husband, Prince Albert, in 1861.

muslin: A sturdy, loosely woven cotton fabric, originally from Bengal, India.

nylon: A durable, synthetic (man-made) fabric invented in 1939 to replace silk. Used so often for stockings that they came to be known as nylons.

organdy: A sheer fabric made of silk or cotton; often used for party dresses.

Orlon: A stretchy, synthetic (man-made) fabric invented in 1967 that does not have to be sewn but is put together in layers with heat, in a process called lamination.

pantalettes: Ankle-length, narrow pants worn as undergarments in the nineteenth century, often trimmed with lace, ruffles, or embroidery.

Peter Pan collar: A rounded collar on a blouse or dress; worn often in the 1930s.

petticoat: A type of slip worn under a skirt in order to widen it, commonly made of cotton and ruffled.

pinafore: A sleeveless garment resembling an apron, which can be worn as a dress or over one.

plaid: A woven fabric with thick and thin lines that cross over one another at right angles.

pleats: A fold in cloth made by doubling the material upon itself and then pressed or stitched to hold it in place.

pudding cap: A child's hat worn in the seventeenth century; padded to protect against injury.

rayon: A soft, synthetic (man-made) fabric created in the early twentieth century.

romper: A one-piece playsuit for young girls, with short, billowy, bloomer-style pants; first worn in the 1920s.

rosettes: Ornamental pieces of ribbon or fabric gathered to resemble roses.

saddle shoes: Laced shoes, sometimes referred to as Oxford style, usually with white toes and heels but a center color of brown or black; popular for girls and boys in the 1950s.

shirtwaists: Blouses popular in the early twentieth century, with full, puffy sleeves, a high collar, pleats down the front, and a narrow waist. The term later referred to a dress with blouselike bodices and plain, full skirts.

silks: Fine, soft, shiny fabrics made from threads produced by silkworms.

smocking: A technique in which fabric is gathered in a pattern with decorative stitching; often used on the bodice of girls' dresses.

sneakers: Rubber-soled shoes invented in the 1910s, so named because rubber soles created quiet footsteps, allowing one to "sneak" around.

spinning: The process of taking a fibrous material such as wool and twisting the fibers into thread or yarn.

stay: *See* corset

striped: A cloth pattern with long narrow bands of color.

swaddling: The wrapping of an infant with cloth, usually linen, to restrict movement; common in medieval times.

sweatshop: A shop or factory where employees work for long hours under poor conditions and for little pay.

T-strap shoe: A style of dress shoe in which two straps form a T and buckle across the top part of the foot.

taffeta: A crisp, smooth fabric with a slight sheen; used especially for special-occasion blouses and dresses.

tanned: Having gone though the process by which animal hides are turned into leather.

tartan plaid: A plaid pattern (*see* plaid) that refers to a Scottish clan.

textile: Cloth.

tintypes: Early types of photographs made similarly to *ambrotypes,* except with thin metal plates instead of glass plates.

tucks: A gathering of material with stitches.

tunic: A long blouse that drops below the waist, usually worn over a skirt. In ancient Greece and Rome, tunics, loose-fitting garments extending to the knees, were worn by both men and women.

tweed: A woven wool pattern, often heavy and nubby, consisting of several colors; commonly used for coats and suits.

velvets: Soft, thick fabrics made of cotton, silk, or a synthetic (man-made) fiber such as rayon or nylon; considered luxurious.

weaving: A process of making cloth in which fibers are interlaced at right angles on a loom.

yarn: A thick, strong strand of twisted fibers.

yoke dresses: Dresses in which the shoulders are fitted and gathers or pleats are formed above the breasts, creating free-flowing skirts.

Bibliography

Agins, Teri. *The End of Fashion: The Mass Marketing of the Clothing Business.* New York: William Morrow, 1999.

Aries, Philippe. *Centuries of Childhood: A Social History of Family Life.* Translated by Robert Baldich. New York: Vintage, 1962.

Bartoletti, Susan Campbell. *Kids on Strike!* Boston: Houghton Mifflin, 1999.

Bishop, Robert. *Folk Painters of America.* New York: Dutton, 1979.

Bissonnette, Anne. *Centuries of Childhood.* On-line catalog. Kent, Ohio: Kent State University Museum, September 27, 2000–September 31, 2001.

Coleridge, Nicholas. *The Fashion Conspiracy.* New York: Harper & Row, 1988.

Dash, Joan. *We Shall Not Be Moved: The Women's Factory Strike of 1909.* New York: Scholastic, 1996.

Deitch, JoAnne Weisman, ed. *The Lowell Mill Girls: Life in the Factory.* Carlisle, Mass.: Discovery Enterprises, 1998.

Foner, Philip S., ed. *The Factory Girls.* Urbana, Ill.: University of Illinois Press, 1977.

———. *Women and the American Labor Movement from Colonial Times to the Eve of World War I.* New York: Free Press, 1979.

Frank, Dana. *Buy American: The Untold Story of Economic Nationalism.* Boston: Beacon Press, 1999.

Freedman, Russell. *Kids at Work: Lewis Hine and the Crusade Against Child Labor.* New York: Clarion, 1994.

Gourley, Catherine. *Good Girl Work: Factories, Sweatshops, and How Women Changed Their Role in the American Workforce.* Brookfield, Conn.: Millbrook Press, 1999.

Green, Harvey. *The Light of the Home: An Intimate View of the Lives of Women in Victorian America.* New York: Pantheon, 1983.

Handlin, Mary F., and Oscar. *Facing Life: Youth and the Family in American History.* Boston: Little, Brown, 1971.

Hefflefinger, Jane, and Elaine Hoffman. *A Hundred Dresses at a Time.* Chicago: Children's Press, 1970.

Humm, Rosamund Olmsted. *Children in America: A Study of Images and Attitudes.* Catalog. Atlanta, Ga.: High Museum of Art, September 30, 1978–May 27, 1979.

Jarnow, Jeanette A., Beatrice Judelle, and Miriam Guerreiro. *Inside the Fashion Business: Text and Readings.* New York: John Wiley & Sons, 1965, 1974, 1981.

Kismaric, Carole, and Marvin Heiferman. *Growing Up with Dick and Jane: Learning and Living the American Dream.* New York: HarperCollins, 1996.

Murray, Maggie Pexton. *Changing Styles in Fashion: Who, What, Why.* Los Angeles: Fashion Institute of Design and Merchandising; New York: Fairchild Publications, 1989.

Panati, Charles. *Panati's Extraordinary Origins of Everyday Things.* New York: Harper & Row, 1987.

Paterson, Katherine. *Lyddie.* New York: Puffin, 1991.

Ross, Andrew, ed. *No Sweat: Fashion, Free Trade, and the Rights of Garment Workers.* New York: Verso, 1997.

Rossner, Judith. *Emmeline.* New York: Simon & Schuster, 1980.

Rubenstein, Ruth P. *Society's Child: Identity, Clothing, and Style.* Boulder, Colo.: Westview Press, 2000.

Schorsch, Anita. *Images of Childhood: An Illustrated Social History.* New York: Mayflower, 1979.

Severa, Joan. *Dressed for the Photographer: Ordinary Americans & Fashion, 1840–1900.* Kent, Ohio: Kent State University Press, 1995.

Smith, Elizabeth Simpson. *Cloth: Inventions That Changed Our Lives.* New York: Walker, 1985.

Underhill, Paco. *Why We Buy: The Science of Shopping.* New York: Simon & Schuster, 1999.

Wertheimer, Barbara Mayer. *We Were There: The Story of Working Women in America.* New York: Pantheon, 1977.

Worrell, Estelle Ansley. *American Costume 1840–1920.* Harrisburg, Pa.: Stackpole, 1979.

Wycoff, Alexander, ed. *The History of American Dress.* N.p.: Benjamin Blom, 1965.

Webography

Textile and Costume Collections on the Internet
Beverly Birks Couture Collection
http://www.camrax.com/pages/birks0.htm
An on-line collection of more than 1,300 images

Cornell Costume and Textile Collection
http://www.human.cornell.edu/txa/cu_costume.cfm
Full on-line catalog with more than 4,000 objects

Helen Louise Allen Textile Collection
University of Wisconsin, Madison
http://sohe.wisc.edu/hlatc/
Information about the collection, including visuals

Historic Costume and Textiles Collection
Ohio State University, Columbus, Ohio
http://costume.osu.edu
Selections from current exhibitions

History Museums and Historical Societies
Darien Historical Society, Darien, Connecticut
http://historical.darien.org

Visual images of selections from the collection

Kent State University Museum
Bissonnette on Costume:
A Visual Dictionary of Fashion
http://dept.kent.edu/museum/costume/
An on-line visual dictionary of fashion

Louisiana State Museum, New Orleans, Louisiana
http://www.lsm.crt.state.la.us/
On-line exhibits

The Metropolitan Museum of Art: The Costume Institute
www.metmuseum.org/Works_of_Art/department.asp?dep=8
Selections from the permanent collection

The Museum at the Fashion Institute of Technology
www.fitnyc.edu/Museum
Selections from current exhibitions

Museums

Costume Institute
The Metropolitan Museum of Art
1000 5th Avenue
New York, NY 10028
212-535-7710

Historic Costume & Textile Collection
Ohio State University
College of Human Ecology
175 Campbell Hall
1787 Neil Avenue
Columbus, OH 43210-129
614-292-3090

Hope B. McCormick Costume Center
Chicago Historical Society
Clark Street at North Avenue
Chicago, IL 60614-6071
312-642-4600

Kent State University Museum
P. O. Box 5190
Rockwell Hall
Kent, OH 44242-0001
330-672-3450

Los Angeles County Museum of Art
5905 Wilshire Boulevard
Los Angeles, CA 90036
323-857-6000

Museum of the City of New York
1220 5th Avenue at 103rd Street
New York, NY 10029
212-534-1672

Museum of the Fashion Institute
of Technology
7th Avenue at 27th Street
New York, NY 10001
212-217-5800

Museum of Fine Arts
465 Huntington Avenue
Boston, MA 02115
617-267-9300

National Gallery of Art & Costume
Design
Between 4th and 9th Streets
at Constitution Avenue NW
Washington, DC 20565
202-737-4215

National Museum
of American History
Smithsonian Institution
14th Street and Constitution Avenue NW
Washington, DC 20001
202-633-1000

Peabody Essex Museum
East India Square
Salem, MA 01970-3783
978-745-9500

Rhode Island School
of Design Museum
224 Benefit Street
Providence, RI 02903
401-454-6500

Texas Fashion Collection
University of North Texas
P. O. Box 305100
Scoular Hall
Denton, TX 76203-5100
940-565-2732

The Textile and Costume Institute
Museum of Fine Arts
5601 Main Street
Houston, TX 77005
713-639-7300

The Textile Museum
2320 South Street NW
Washington, DC 20008-4088
202-667-0441

U.S. Army Women's Museum
2100 Adams Avenue
Building P-5219
Fort Lee, VA 23801-2100
(804)734-4327

The Valentine Museum
1015 East Clay Street
Richmond, VA 23219
(804) 649-0711

The Wages Collection
One Centennial Circle
Gainsville, GA 30501
(770) 534-6244

Organizations

These are organizations that provide information about and support or promote fair labor practices in the textile industry.

Co-op America
1612 K Street NW

Suite 600
Washington, DC 20006
800-584-7336

U. S. Department of Labor
200 Constitution Avenue NW
Washington, DC 20210
866-4-USA-DOL

National Consumers' League/
Child Labor Coalition
1701 K Street NW
Suite 1200
Washington, DC 20006
202-835-3323
www.stopchildlabor.org/

National Labor Committee
540 West 48th Street
New York, NY 10036
212-242-3002

National Mobilization Against
Sweatshops
P. O. Box 130293
New York, NY 10013-0995
www.nmass.org

Smithsonian Museum Exhibition

http://Americanhistory.si.edu/
sweatshops
Sweatshop Watch
10 Eighth Street
Suite 303
Oakland, CA 94607
510-834-8990
www.sweatshopwatch.org

UNITE
275 7th Avenue
New York, NY 10011
212-265-7000
www.UNITEunion.org

United Students Against Sweatshops
1150 17th Street NW
Suite 300
Washington, DC 20036
202-NO-SWEAT

Wear Fair
606 Shaw Street
Toronto ON M6G 3L6
Canada
perg@web.net

Art Credits

Index

Page numbers in *italics* refer to illustrations